What *Fathers* Are

PHOTOGRAPHS BY LAURA STRAUS

Ariel Books

**Andrews McMeel
Publishing**

Kansas City

Photographs copyright © 2002 by Laura Straus, NY

Edited by Susan Feuer, Kelli Giammarco, and Cassandra Khan

ISBN: 0-7407-2271-9

Library of Congress Catalog Card Number: 2001096370

preface Using the camera as my guide, I have explored the different aspects of friendship in the book *What Girlfriends Do*, the relationship of a mother to her child in *What Mothers Are*, the connection between couples in *What Love Is*, the fun shared by teenage girls in *Girls, Girls, Girls*, and the magic of childhood in *A Child's World*. Each book has provided me with the opportunity to explore these relationships and see them through different eyes—and so it is for this book, *What Fathers Are*.

Here, then, is a vision of today's father. He is the multifaceted man at the center of the gentle Smith family, the warm and energetic father of the Green family, and the compassionate father of the Fabricant family. You will meet the great open-armed snugglers of the Gaffney and Wright families, and the nurturing warmth of the Bradley family.

I got to know my own father best late in life. We both became photographers, also late in life. It has been his support, his guidance, and most of all his good counsel that has helped me to believe in myself as a photographer. These photographs are a testament to his gift as a teacher. I still turn to him weekly for guidance. This book is dedicated to Roger Straus III, and to all of our dads!

—Laura Straus

What fathers

a warm presence

good listeners

guardians

the best mates

there to lean on

patient

good providers

true companions

captivated

whirlwinds of fun

in the thick of it all

uplifting

handy

devoted

kids at heart

supportive

mentors

proud

*shelter from
the storm*

reflective _____

fun-loving

close at hand

all-embracing

reliable _____

playful

sporting

nurturing

bear huggers _____

creative

behind us
all the way

This book was designed by BTDnyc

. . . AND TYPESET BY BTDNYC IN DUCHAMP BOLD AND SABON.